Original title:
The Glow of Winter Twilight

Author: Aurora Sinclair

ISBN HARDBACK: 978-9916-94-616-9
ISBN PAPERBACK: 978-9916-94-617-6

Enchanted Hues of a Fading Day

The sun slips down, a golden slip,
Bouncing on clouds like a froggy flip.
The snowflakes laugh as they start to fall,
Tickling our noses, oh, what a ball.

Children run, with scarves untied,
Chasing shadows, full of pride.
The sky wears purple, pink, and blue,
As rosy cheeks say, "Look at you!"

Serene Encounters at Day's End

A penguin waddles, slips, then zooms,
With snowball fights and giggling blooms.
A squirrel darts with an acorn stash,
Jetting around in a frenzied dash.

Mittens on paws, they catch and throw,
Grinning wide as chill winds blow.
A snowman grins, with a cheeky grin,
As if to say, "Let the fun begin!"

Mistletoe Dreams Under Starlit Canopies

In the glen, where the twinklers gleam,
Crafty raccoons plot and scheme.
Foxes prance, wearing hats askew,
Koalas chime in, singing too.

Beneath the boughs, under frosty sights,
Dance a waltz, all in their tights.
The mistletoe sways, oh what a tease,
Promising kisses with winter breeze.

Whispers of Ghostly Light on Snow

A ghostly owl hoots, quite bizarre,
Wearing a scarf from the local bazaar.
His floppy hat flops side to side,
As he eyes the snowman, soon to slide.

The moonlight giggles, reflecting the glow,
On frosty flakes that twirl below.
All critters gather, a hilarious mess,
To see who can make the biggest dress!

Nightfall's Caress on a Frigid Eve

Snowflakes tumble, dance in glee,
While squirrels wear scarves, sipping tea.
A snowman winks with a carrot nose,
Says, "I'm cooler than anyone knows!"

Chilly breezes play hide and seek,
As penguins strut in their tails so sleek.
The frost makes noses turn bright red,
While kids giggle, their fingers sled!"

Softly Glimmering Souls of the Cold

Icicles dangle like playful swords,
While reindeer play cards and swap their hoards.
A lazy cat purrs beside the fire,
Dreaming of fish that never tire.

Footprints in snow form a silly line,
As penguins execute a perfect sign.
With snowballs flying in a playful fight,
Winter laughs at silly delights!

Secrets Shared at the Edge of Twilight

Gossiping trees whisper in the chill,
While snowmen tell tales with unstoppable will.
A frozen lake reflects silly pranks,
As frostbite makes it hard to give thanks.

Elves dressed in sweaters, with nimble toes,
Dance to tunes that nobody knows.
Huddled creatures share a cup of cheer,
Wishing for warmth as the night draws near!

Whispers of Frosted Dusk

Under the stars, the owls give a hoot,
While rabbits wear hats in their fuzzy suit.
The moon chuckles at the frozen spree,
It's just another night for you and me!

Winter's charm with a frosty grin,
Inviting all to bring the fun within.
Sipping cocoa, we snicker and snort,
Finding joy in this chilly court!

Embrace of a Quiet Winter Night

Snowflakes fall like silent clowns,
Dressing up our little town.
Squirrels in hats, a sight so rare,
Jokes exchanged in frosty air.

Children giggle as they slip,
On the ice, they take a dip.
Snowmen sport a frosty grin,
While cats plot their sneaky sins.

Hot cocoa warms cold fingers tight,
As marshmallows take a flight.
Dreams of sledding fill the room,
While daylight's lost to evening gloom.

Crystalline Melodies of Solstice

Icicles play a tune of glee,
Humming softly, can't you see?
Frosty winds whisper to the trees,
A cheerful dance on frosted breeze.

Penguins in boots, they strut around,
In a winter parade, so proud and sound.
Snowballs fly like popcorn tossed,
Laughter echoes, never lost.

Coffee mugs clink, a warm embrace,
As snowflakes drift, they pick up pace.
A wink from the moon, oh what a sight,
While we twirl in the sparkling night.

Awash in Twilight's Serenity

Twilight falls like a velvet cloak,
Covering mischief, a gentle joke.
Winter critters don their jammies,
Sharing secrets, their funny shammies.

A cat in a scarf, oh so chic,
Stumbles over its paws, what a peak!
Snowmen gossip, their noses bright,
As giggles dance through the cold night.

A whisper of chill, the moon takes flight,
Bringing stories wrapped up tight.
Cozy fires crackle, warmth we share,
Creating laughter in the frosty air.

Fluff of Gentle White Dreams

Pillow fights in snowy flurries,
Bumbling through the soft, white curries.
Fluffy boots stomp as kids rejoice,
With giggles ringing, they raise their voice.

Snowflakes tickle as they fall,
A playful race, we've won them all.
Hot pies bake a savory tune,
While snowmen dance beneath the moon.

A cheeky fox with a carrot nose,
Tries to sneak away, oh who knows?
But laughter fills the starry night,
As friends chase shadows, hearts alight.

A Dance of Frost and Fading Sun

As sunlight winks, the shadows play,
Snowflakes bring a cheer today.
The squirrels scamper, looking for treats,
Chasing their tails on tiny feet.

A snowman wobbles, one eye askew,
He tips his hat, says, "How do you do?"
Kids in mittens throw snowy balls,
While the frostbite laughs and gently calls.

Reflections in a Shimmering Twilight

The sky's a canvas, pink and blue,
A disco ball with a frosty hue.
Snowy owls hoot a turtleneck tune,
As rabbits dance under the moon.

A hot cocoa mustache, oh what a sight,
Slippery steps, oh what a fright!
With each giggle, the cold seems less,
Winter chuckles in its fluffy dress.

Veiled in Radiance of Winter's Breath

Icicles hang like shiny blades,
While kids in snow, attempt parades.
The winter rug rats throw a fit,
Muffins with snow make a gooey split.

The warm socks wander, so mismatched,
In a frosty game, they are attached.
Laughter rings loud, a happy sound,
As tumbleweeds of snow swirl round.

Celestial Glow in the Heart of Winter

Under lights that twinkle bright,
Reindeer in sweaters take their flight.
A snowball flies, a comical sight,
Hits a dad, oh what a plight!

The flurries spin like giggling sprites,
Frosty breath puts up small fights.
With every slip, there's laughs to store,
Winter's jesters, begging for more!

A Glimpse of Starlit Tranquility

In frosty air, the snowmen grinned,
With carrot noses, their dreams begin.
They danced on ice, a wobbly show,
While playful squirrels were stealing the snow.

A cat in boots, with swagger so bold,
Challenged the winter, fierce and cold.
But slipped on ice and tumbled down,
A fluffy butterball, wearing a frown.

Serene Horizons in Winter's Embrace

The snowflakes fell like tiny jokes,
Wrapping trees like silly cloaks.
As pine trees shook, their needles sneezed,
While children laughed, their cheeks were pleased.

A penguin slipped, went for a ride,
Down a snowy hill, with joy and pride.
His friends just laughed, a giddy crew,
As snowballs flew, and chaos grew.

Judicious Hues Beneath a Cold Sky

Colors of twilight, pink and blue,
The snowflakes swirling, a whimsical view.
A moose on skates, in dramatic fashion,
Twirled and leaped, creating a splashin'.

Fluffy clouds like cotton candy spun,
While reindeer giggled, having their fun.
But mistletoe fell, kissed a tree,
Oh look, a squirrel, as sweet as can be!

Last Flickers Before Solitude

In winter's clutch, the fireflies blink,
Their light a laugh, don’t you think?
Chasing shadows, they dashed through the night,
While hibernating bears dreamed of a bite.

An icicle dripped, made a splashy sound,
As penguins waddled, joyfully round.
The moon peeked out, in a goofball spree,
Stars giggled softly, oh what a sight to see!

Whispering Pines Beneath Frosty Skies

Pines wear coats of sparkling white,
They giggle as the stars ignite.
Frosty breath on frosty ground,
Squirrels chase, their laughter sound.

Snowflakes dance like feathered sprites,
On chilly winds, they take their flights.
A rabbit slips, a tumbly fall,
Snowman chuckles, he can't stand tall.

A Delicate Kiss from a Dimming Sun

As daylight winks, it trips the light,
The sun gives twilight a playful bite.
Snowballs in the air, a frosty brawl,
Come join the fun, don't miss the call!

Chasing shadows in the fading glow,
They leap and bob, like puppets in tow.
A snowflake lands upon my nose,
And suddenly, a snow-cream froze.

Shadows Play in the Arctic Gloam

In evening's lap, where shadows prance,
They whisper secrets with a glance.
A polar bear in a tutu spins,
While snowmen dance with goofy grins.

A trio of owls hoot a tune,
As laughter echoes 'neath the moon.
Wild rabbits form a line to hop,
In a frosty conga, they won't stop!

Hushed Tales Beneath the Winter Sky

Stars twinkle tales of mischief bright,
While secret snowflakes prepare to write.
A sled glides down with boisterous cheer,
And snowmen slam-dunk a snowball beer.

Icicles hang like frozen spears,
They drip and clink, echoing cheers.
Beneath the trees, the critters play,
As winter whispers at the end of day.

Breathing in the Night’s Solstice

Snowflakes twirl like dancers in flight,
A snowman’s hat flies off in delight.
The rabbits hop, looking for cheer,
While squirrels are plotting their nutty beer.

Chill air tickles noses, oh what a tease,
Penguins in scarves say, "Brrr, if you please!"
Hot cocoa spills, a marshmallow flood,
Laughter erupts over frozen mud.

Nature's Quiet Refrain

Trees wrapped in blankets, cozy and snug,
Birds wear their mittens, all warm and smug.
The brook whispers tales as it glitters and wiggles,
While owls hoot softly, throwing out giggles.

Bears snooze away, wrapped in their dreams,
While raccoons plot heists with mischievous schemes.
Icicles dangle like chandeliers grand,
But if they could talk, they’d call for a band.

Dappled Light of the Fading Sun

The sun wears a cloak of soft purple hue,
Bouncing off snow like a clown at the zoo.
Footprints lead nowhere, what a funny sight,
A penguin parade, waddling with might.

The rabbits are hopping, pulling their pranks,
While the deer take a bow, giving their thanks.
Funny hats made of pine cones they sport,
Nature's own circus, a slapstick report.

Cadence of Silence Wrapped in Frost

Frost paints the windows, a crafty delight,
Chasing cats like they're caught in a fight.
While snowmen gossip about carrot-nosed fame,
They chuckle and whisper, playing a game.

The moon peeks in, with a grin so wide,
As penguins slip-slide, trying to hide.
Whispers of winter, with a giggle or two,
In this frosty realm, there's laughter anew.

Hushed Bliss of the Evening

Snowflakes dance like playful flies,
Chasing each other across the skies.
A penguin tries to slide and fails,
Wobbles off the path, tails like trails.

Hot cocoa spills upon my mittens,
While laughing squirrels plan their missions.
Frosted trees wear coats of white,
And I trip over my own delight.

The moon sneezes at the chilly air,
While bunnies hop without a care.
Chasing shadows that skip and leap,
In this frosty fun, we laugh and creep.

With each giggle, the night grows bright,
As snowflakes gather, what a sight!
Evening hush holds muffled cheer,
In this silly land of winter sheer.

Starry Evenings Draped in White

Stars peek out like eyes on high,
Adventurous voices start to fly.
A dog barks at the silent moon,
While snowflakes fall, we’ll sing a tune.

Jack Frost nibbles on my nose,
Creating frosty, funny prose.
Fluffy clouds, where snowmen hide,
Join snowy cars on a slippery ride.

Kittens tumble in frozen glee,
As snowballs fly like sparks from me.
Surprises lurk in snowy piles,
A winter wonderland of smiles.

Even the owls have cracked a joke,
While snowy trees begin to poke.
Laughing together, against the chill,
In a snowy world, we can't sit still!

Twilight's Painted Whispers

The sunset paints the sky with cheer,
As chilly breezes tickle my ear.
Snowmen gossip with wise old trees,
Wishing for hot chocolate, if you please.

A rabbit dons its fluffy scarf,
While snowflakes cause a winter laugh.
Ducks waddle by with ruffled flair,
Pretending they're ladies at a fair.

Under the stars, the jokes run wild,
As kittens bounce like a playful child.
Beneath the twinkle, warmth can glow,
In this frosty fiesta, let it flow!

With each chuckle, we shiver bright,
In snowy mischief that feels just right.
As twilight whispers softly near,
We'll dance along without a fear.

Frostbitten Dreams of Tranquility

Dreams wrapped up in scarves so tight,
Snow angels flail with all their might.
A cat in a sweater, oh what a sight,
Warming up by the firelight.

Frosty windows are a canvas, dear,
Creating laughter as we cheer.
Here comes the snowman with a broom,
Singing songs to the moon’s soft zoom.

Chasing shadows with laughter bold,
As icy tales of fun unfold.
A chicken in mittens trots along,
With feathers fluffed for winter's song.

Even the icicles seem to sway,
As snowflakes dance and fly away.
In dreams of frost, we're wild and free,
In this quiet chaos, just you and me.

Variegated Evening Glow

The sun dips low, calls it a day,
Snowmen argue, who's got the sway.
Scarves wrapped tight, they wobble and dance,
Sleds careen, a frostbitten prance.

Hot cocoa spills, a chocolate war,
Marshmallow grenades fly from the floor.
Chasing snowflakes, they trip and tumble,
Laughter bursts, as giggles rumble.

Trees in their coats, sparkling bright,
Giggles echo through the cold night.
Snowflakes settle on noses and hats,
While snowmen plot like affable brats.

Laughter rings sharp in the frosty air,
Winter's charm can't help but declare.
With every slip and tumbling cheer,
Joy lights the dark, winter's premiere.

Emblems of Celestial Quiet

Stars blink down in their jolly array,
Whispers of snowflakes dance and sway.
While squirrels stash nuts in snow-covered hills,
A chorus of critters share wintery thrills.

The moon grins wide, a big, shiny face,
Bunnies in scarves hop, keep up the pace.
Laughter erupts with a soft little thud,
As snowballs fly through a flurry of fun.

Frost on the windows paints pictures of glee,
While kittens pounce in the chestnut tree.
Icicles dangle, drippity-drop,
And snow drifts silently, until they stop.

Each moment sparkles with whimsy and cheer,
As winter's laughter is finally here.
In this frosty realm, where fun never quits,
Even the moon knows where the giggle fits.

Frostwoven Nightfall

Clouds quilt the skies, drifting snug and slow,
While snowflakes twirl in a frosty tableau.
Chill in the air, but hearts are ablaze,
Tickled by winter's amusing phase.

Penguins in bowties waddle with pride,
Holding snowball fights their friends can’t abide.
Ice skates whirl, as folks glide by,
And merry hearts laugh, forgetting to sigh.

Mittens and boots make quite the parade,
Kidding the snowmen who feel a bit frayed.
Every stumble brings boisterous mirth,
As chilly embraces affirm winter's birth.

Stars wink from above, twinkling with glee,
Critters rejoice in this choreographed spree.
Winter's embrace may be chilly and bright,
But jovial souls keep the warmth in sight!

Echoes of the Icy Twilight

Hilarity reigns in the fading light,
As snowflakes wobble in a comical flight.
Gloves mismatched, boots all askew,
Chasing their shadows; oh, what a view!

The frost bites back with a grin of its own,
As friends share giggles over ice cream cones.
From snowball duels to fort-building schemes,
Each twist and turn feeds into their dreams.

Whispers of laughter float on the breeze,
While children pile high their powdered cheese.
Frosty fingers cling to taunting snow,
Hilarity grows as the twilight glow.

Under the stars, with hearts ever light,
Chasing the dusk, embracing the night.
In winter's embrace, we find our delight,
As echoes of joy magnify the twilight.

Melodies of Icy Calm

Snowflakes dance, twirling down,
A penguin slips, wears a frown.
Hot cocoa spills, marshmallows fly,
Laughter echoes, oh my, oh my!

Squirrels race on branches tall,
One falls down, gives it his all.
Chasing after a nut so grand,
Slips again—oh, isn't life bland?

Frosty breath and icy air,
A snowman's hat held with a prayer.
He sneezes loud, it's quite a sight,
Losing a carrot in the night!

Bundled up in silly gear,
A dog runs past, gives a cheer.
Chasing tails in snowflakes bright,
Winter fun, what pure delight!

Chasing the Last Light

Bats wear capes, adjusting style,
Trying hard to chirp with guile.
Sunset fades into a giggle,
The golden hues give us a wiggle.

A snowman winks, he’s feeling bold,
Wearing shades, if truth be told.
Winter sun dances on the snow,
“Catch me quick!” it seems to glow.

A squirrel hums, doing a jig,
In fluffy boots, it seems so big.
With mittens made of dishcloth thread,
His winter dance, a sight to spread!

Rabbits plotting a daring heist,
Nibbling carrots, now that’s spice!
Sunset giggles, takes a dip,
Leaving chuckles on every lip!

Bated Breath of Nightfall

Stars come out, like cheeky sprites,
While owls hoot their funny rights.
A cat in boots struts with flair,
Chasing shadows, unaware!

The moon slips in with a wink so sly,
Casting laughs across the sky.
Snow crunches under feet, a beat,
As mischief scurries on, oh sweet!

A raccoon dons a shiny mask,
Planning pranks—oh what a task!
"Do not disturb," he signs at night,
While giggling softly, what a fright!

Wrapped in blankets, folks behold,
Stories shared, both silly and bold.
Frozen giggles float on high,
Nightfall holds the loudest sigh!

Night’s Crystal Promise

Icicles hang, like treacherous swords,
While snowflakes fall in soft, sweet hoards.
They tickle noses, make us sneeze,
Winter’s antics don’t aim to please!

A dog rolls ‘round with a gleeful bark,
Wearing a hat, it’s quite the lark!
Chasing tails in a flurry of fun,
With each escapade, he’s never done!

Chimneys puff, a smoke signal speaks,
Telling tales of frosty peaks.
Mittens missing, fashion faux pas,
Laughing together, it’s winter law!

Starlit sky, a blanket of glee,
While cocoa dreams steep endlessly.
With a wink, the night takes its bow,
Winter’s whispers promise somehow!

Evening's Glistening Embrace

Snowflakes dance like awkward mice,
Noses pink, oh what a price!
Chasing sleds down hills with glee,
We tumble down, oh woe is me!

Hot cocoa spills, a frothy mess,
Marshmallows float, a sweet caress.
Giggles echo from the trees,
While icicles dangle with a sneeze!

Laughter wraps like a warm blanket,
In mittened hands, we make a prank yet.
Snowman grins with a crooked hat,
Oh, whoever thought of that!

As night creeps in, we prance about,
In the cold, our voices shout.

Twilight’s Shimmering Veil

The sun waves bye with a cheeky grin,
Daytime mischief is hard to pin.
As shadows stretch and giggle too,
We hop along, 'What will we do?'

Snowmen play hide and seek with the stars,
While snowballs sail like tiny cars.
Frosty eyebrows raise in glee,
Winter’s jesters, wild and free!

Laughter bounces, a merry song,
Jackets zipped, we thrill along.
The chilly breeze whispers a tale,
Of flurries swirling, a dazzling veil.

Under the moon’s watchful eye,
We make funny faces, oh my, oh my!
Twilight winks in a frosty dance,
Come join us for a winter prance!

Celestial Reflections on Snow

Stars twinkle like candy in the sky,
We skate on ice, giving it a try.
With every slip, a loud hooray,
Winter's stage is our cabaret!

The snowman wears a scarf so bright,
While penguins slide with pure delight.
Sleds zoom past in a hasty rush,
As we cheer, 'Hold on, don’t mush!'

Jingle bells echo through the town,
As snowflakes tumble, never frown.
We build a fort, as strong as can be,
The only rule: throw snow at me!

The moon giggles at our snowy jest,
In winter's chill, we feel so blessed.
Under the starlit blanket, we play,
In this winter wonder, we laugh all day!

Twilight's Embrace of Stillness

Beneath the sky all shades of blue,
Children shriek and build anew.
A snowball flops right in my face,
In this stillness, there’s such grace!

The air is crisp, our cheeks aglow,
Wooly hats high, what a show!
Sleds zoom past, a wild affair,
As we hurl snowflakes without a care!

Candles flicker from cozy sights,
We roast marshmallows, oh what bites!
Our snowmen wink, who made their nose?
Carrot mishaps, it surely shows!

As twilight settles, laughter glows,
Winter’s chime is what we chose.
In this wonderland of gleeful bliss,
We dance ‘neath stars, a frosty kiss!

Periwinkle Dreams Unfolded

In scarves and mittens, they dance with glee,
Frolicking snowflakes, wild as can be.
A penguin in slippers, sliding with style,
Winter's sweet madness, brightening a mile.

Hot cocoa spills over, marshmallows collide,
The snowman’s top hat is on quite a ride.
With noses like carrots, grinning so wide,
They're plotting to snowball, no fear to hide.

Sleds zooming downhill, pure chaos in sight,
A cat in a beanie offers a fright.
Laughter erupts when the ground takes a dip,
As mittens go flying from a daring trip.

Yet in this cool chaos, joy takes its seat,
With snowball fights brewing, it's hard to beat.
Periwinkle dreams drift, silent and bold,
As winter’s own jesters weave stories untold.

Subtle Glimmers of Hibernation

The squirrels are plotting behind the brown trees,
Taking notes in a notebook, preparing the tease.
While rabbits in burrows dream up their schemes,
Fluffy ideas make way for silly dreams.

A hedgehog in slippers, tiptoeing around,
Finds a stash of acorns, no doubt underground.
And bears in pajamas, snoring with flair,
Only waking for snacks they can find anywhere.

Whispers of winter hide under the frost,
While mugs of hot cider are never quite lost.
Pillow forts pop up in the soft falling night,
With whispers of cuddles, it feels so just right.

As chimneys puff smoke, in a dance with the sky,
Chasing frosty wishes, the giggles come by.
The world in still slumber, yet laughter is keen,
In this magical kingdom, it’s all quite serene.

An Ode to Frosted Serenades

Beneath frosty twinkle, the snowflakes declare,
A concert of giggles floats fresh in the air.
The wind plays a tune on the trees with a grin,
While penguins on ice are attempting a spin.

With boots full of snow, and laughter on lips,
The children are singing while doing wild flips.
They tumble and roll, as the cold starts to bite,
With snow men taking notes, it’s a glorious sight.

Caught in a snowstorm, a cat gets a fright,
As snow sprays the streets in a glittery white.
Yet see how it purrs, all bundled so tight,
A fuzzy delight in the cold of the night.

Chasing the shadows with giggles and cheer,
As winter serenades bring strangers so near.
This ode lingers sweetly, like sugar on ice,
In frosted enchantment, all things feel so nice.

Midnight’s Subdued Glint

As night softly blankets the world in a hush,
Snowman shows up for a late-night plush.
He brings marshmallow snacks and a twinkle of fun,
With giggles and laughter, side-splitting runs.

The owls start to hoot, but the raccoons cheer loud,
Hosting a party, tucked under a cloud.
With cupcakes of snow and a punch made of ice,
Even stars wink and tease with some playful advice.

The moon looks bemused at the antics below,
Why do they leap like they’re dancing in snow?
But they frolic and tumble, all carefree and bright,
Chasing bubbles of giggles in the soft evening light.

So let the frost twinkle, and let laughter soar,
In this merry moonlight, who could ask for more?
Each snicker and giggle, a glimmering treat,
As midnight’s sly glint makes winter complete.

Silhouettes in Indigo

In the dusk, the squirrels play,
Wearing tiny hats, they sway.
Snowflakes dance, they trip and spin,
While giggling birds all join in.

Trees wear scarves, a frosty cheer,
Whispering jokes for all to hear.
A rabbit hops with a jaunty bow,
In a world that's snowy and somehow foul.

Street lamps blink in a comicalight,
A flicker here, a funny sight.
As shadows stretch and twist with glee,
Even the moon is chuckling, whee!

So let's embrace this silly scene,
With frozen noses, we all glean.
A chuckle shared, a smile so wide,
In lavender hours, let joy reside.

Breaths of Chilled Serenity

Puffs of breath like little clouds,
Turn to snowflakes in tiny crowds.
With noses red and cheeks aglow,
Who knew winter could put on a show?

Frosty windows draw goofy shapes,
While icicles form as silly drapes.
A snowman sports a carrot nose,
And a hat that blows when the wind blows.

Chasing snowflakes that start to fall,
While wearing socks that are too small.
A slip and slide, a tumble, a cheer,
Oops! I fell right—into the beer!

We laugh at the chill, embrace the night,
Hot cocoa with marshy delight.
In this cold chaos, we dance and play,
Finding warmth in humor every day.

Luminous Shadows of Evening

A cat prances on a snowy track,
Chasing shadows that playfully crack.
With fluff on his tail, and a meow so sweet,
He leaps through the drifts, oh such a feat!

Snowflakes giggle as they descend,
It's a snowball fight with no clear end.
With hats askew and mittens misfit,
Laughter echoes in every bit.

Cars twinkling like stars in a dance,
But someone's stuck—oh, what a chance!
With a honk and a shout, it's a candy cane race,
A winter wonderland, oh, what a place!

So here's to the night, full of giggles and grins,
As frost paints the world with silly spins.
We'll find joy where shadows can play,
In this whimsical twilight, let's laugh away!

Frost-Laced Horizons

Gazing far at the icy expanse,
Penguins slide in a well-practiced dance.
They twirl and trip on their frosty feet,
As the world around them bursts with beat.

With polar bears wearing snazzy bow ties,
They sway together beneath gray skies.
Each paw print left is a giggle's trace,
In this chilly kingdom, what a wild place!

Snow cones form on the trees up high,
As snowflakes twinkle like stars in the sky.
Elk in tuxedos strut with flair,
While all of nature stops and stares.

So raise a glass of hot tea and cheer,
To the madness that brings us all here.
In cold's embrace, let laughter thrive,
In frost-laced horizons, we come alive!

Afterglow of a Whispering Sky

A snowman wears a hat too big,
He trips and lands right on a twig.
The stars above all start to laugh,
As snowflakes dance like a comic half.

The moon's a funny face tonight,
With cheesy grins, it brings delight.
The chill in air starts to tease,
While snowballs fly with careless ease.

A penguin slides down icy trails,
While rabbits plot their winter jails.
The squirrels giggle in high branches,
As winter drapes us in its trances.

With furry hats and purple socks,
We skate on ice, our feet like rocks.
The evening hums a quirky tune,
As twilight whispers to the moon.

Hushed Murmurs of Fading Day

In cozy socks, we sip hot cocoa,
The leftovers from last night's hero.
A creature peeks from behind a tree,
It’s just a cat, not a yeti!

The clouds above seem quite absurd,
They look like pillows, not a bird.
A flurry giggles, swirls about,
As snowflakes tease and dance with doubt.

The chilly air is crisp and clear,
While frosty noses bring some cheer.
We throw a snowball, it goes wide,
And lands on Dad, he's not amused inside!

Yet laughter lingers in the chill,
As shadows dance upon the hill.
We greet the night with playful sighs,
And watch the stars twinkle in the skies.

Enigmatic Glistening

The moonlight winks, a playful tease,
Illuminates the frosted trees.
A rabbit hops with clumsy pride,
While chasing shadows, taking a ride.

Each snowflake falls with a little joke,
Even the pine trees start to poke.
The frost does giggle on the glass,
As twilight colors come to pass.

A frosty breath can turn to steam,
As if the night has lost its theme.
The owls roll eyes at toasty snacks,
As winter's whimsy sneaks in cracks.

With bubbling laughter, we adore,
The quirky antics, fun and more.
We gather close, as fires glow bright,
And celebrate the joy of night.

Flurries of Colored Spaciousness

The skies above wear purple hues,
While quirky birds exchange their views.
A snowman starts to lose his head,
Too much laughter, enough said!

The ground is carpeted in white,
But colors pop, it feels so right.
The sun sets low with silly cheer,
As giggles echo, drawing near.

The winter's chill brings frosty fun,
Where snowball fights have just begun.
A dog spins round, chasing its tail,
As we all laugh, we cannot fail.

With scarves and mittens, joy abounds,
Under pink clouds, in playful bounds.
In every flurry, laughter grows,
As winter whispers all it knows.

Lullabies of Light and Snowdrift Dreams

In the land where snowflakes dance and prance,
Even snowmen join in a wacky chance.
They tip their hats and give a jig,
While squirrels wear socks and do a big gig.

Under stars with secret dreams to share,
The penguins throw parties without a care.
Snowballs are thrown with a giggly cheer,
As we sip hot cocoa by the fireplace, dear.

Frosty whispers lull the night so bright,
While fluffy blankets hug us tight,
We count the sheep, or maybe some goats,
In a world where the cold brings funny notes.

So laugh away, as winter's wonder grows,
With snowman tales and frosty throws.
In this crystal land where joy takes flight,
We find our fun in the cheeky night.

Fading Warmth of the Winter Horizon

The sun creeps low with a sleepy yawn,
As snowflakes laugh, like little elves on lawn.
Chasing their shadows, they slip and slide,
While icy breezes take the winter's ride.

Snowmen gossip in their carrot-nosed glee,
As winter tales unfold, oh so free.
Hot chocolate splashes with whipping cream,
Filling the air with a chocolate dream.

Icicles swing like a band on a spree,
Telling the tales of who got a freeze.
Bunny slippers hop, with a bump and a squeak,
In this frosty land, no day is bleak.

So gather around, while the winter winds sigh,
With mittens and hats, we reach for the sky.
The fading warmth holds a ticklish delight,
As snowmen chuckle in the glowing twilight.

Seraphic Glow of the Frozen Veil

Billowing flakes drift like cotton candy,
While the chill sends giggles that feel quite dandy.
Frosty fairies skip with joyous glee,
Sprinkling laughter, oh, what a spree!

Under the glow of the pale moon’s tease,
Snowflakes play hide and seek in the breeze.
The owls wear scarves made of glittering frost,
As the night wraps us up, never feeling lost.

In cozy corners, where hot pies bake,
We share silly stories by the hearth’s quake.
The cat in a sweater, just can't stop prancing,
While shadows in the nook join in sweet dancing.

So join in the laughter, let worries fly,
With snowmen at play and owls who sigh.
In this frozen veil, where the jests will swirl,
We frolic in joy, let the fun unfurl!

A Reverie of Silvery Light

In a dreamy world where snowflakes play,
Bunnies do cartwheels, oh what a display!
Plump little penguins make snowball forts,
While chatter fills the air with giggly retorts.

Marshmallow clouds float above our heads,
As we toast by the fire, snuggled in beds.
Giggling children sled down hills so wide,
While frosty breath swirls in playful glide.

As the stars twinkle with a wink and a glow,
The mischievous moon keeps putting on a show.
Chasing the shadows in the soft silver night,
We find joy in the snowscape, what a delight!

So sprinkle the giggles, let laughter ignite,
In this charming place, where day meets the night.
In a reverie of dreams, where we lay in the light,
We twirl and we whirl—we're all winter's might!

Frosted Whispers of Dusk

The squirrels in their jackets skate,
On ice so thin, they tempt their fate.
Winter's chill brings a frosty bite,
Yet laughter echoes through the night.

Snowflakes fall like tiny balls,
Each one hints of nature's brawls.
With cheeks like apples, red and bright,
They wrestle shadows in the light.

Icicles hang like crystal spears,
A chandelier of frozen tears.
They shimmer down from rooftops high,
While giggles spark and spirits fly.

But as the dusk begins to bloom,
Their antics fade, a fleeting room.
With crumpets warm and cocoa sweet,
They dream of snow in cozy greet.

Ember Skies and Silent Snow

The sun bids farewell with a wink,
As everyone stops to think,
About the snacks that fill the night,
And snowmen wearing hats so tight.

Fires crackle while raccoons dance,
In flickering flames, they take their chance.
A marshmallow’s plop sings like a tune,
Yet it vanishes before the moon.

In this quiet, each shadow beams,
With dreams of pies and cookie dreams.
The chilly air makes noses red,
As frosty whispers fill your head.

We laugh at flakes that land with grace,
On noses, hats, and every face.
And as we pile the snow up high,
We watch it melt beneath the sky.

Celestial Hues at Dimming Light

The stars peek out, oh what a show,
As rabbits hop in the dimming glow.
Chasing shadows in playful flits,
While snowflakes dance like little skits.

The moon grins down, a cheeky spark,
On frozen ponds where fishes lurk.
With winter's lull, a playful joke,
A snowball flies — oh, what a poke!

In cozy homes, the tales unfold,
Of frosty mischief, legends bold.
While kittens chase their tails in glee,
As laughter swirls like misty tea.

So let’s embrace this capered night,
With every giggle, hold on tight.
For as the twilight plays its part,
We keep the warmth close to our heart.

Twilight's Embrace in Crystal Air

As daylight fades, the fun begins,
With snowball fights and playful spins.
The frosty air, it tickles noses,
While each rebellious flake forecloses.

Snowmen grin with carrot smiles,
While winter’s charm stretches for miles.
Tales of Yeti, big and round,
With snow-muffs lost on frozen ground.

Hot chocolate wars, a frothy race,
As each kiddo fights to claim their place.
With marshmallows puffing, sweet delight,
They toast the season through the night.

So gather 'round the gleaming fire,
As giggles rise ever higher.
For in this chilly, joyous spree,
Winter's fun is wild and free.

Chasing Shadows Beneath Silver Clouds

A penguin waddles, slips and slides,
In search of midnight snacks, she glides.
Snowflakes sparkle like a disco ball,
While snowmen dance, just having a ball!

Bunnies hop with goofy grace,
Chasing shadows in a crazy race.
All the while, the owls hold court,
Laughing at the mixed-up sport.

Sleds tumble down with laughter loud,
Bright red hats on a snowball crowd.
With each fall, they burst with glee,
Winter mischief, oh, so carefree!

So grab your mittens, come join the fun,
Where frosty nights are never done.
In the chilly air, we play and cheer,
Chasing shadows without fear!

Echoes of Frost in the Gathering Dark

A squirrel in a hat, what a sight,
Looking for nuts with all his might.
His chubby cheeks filled to the brim,
While a fox giggles at the whim!

Icicles dangle, like frozen spears,
As snowflakes dance to winter's cheers.
They slip and slide on icy rills,
Laughing while dodging frosty spills!

The moon peeks out, shining bright,
Illuminating every snowy plight.
But here comes a cat, thinking he’s sly,
Chasing shadows that flit and fly.

Oh, the echoes of laughter surround,
As prancing feet make a joyful sound.
In this frosty world, it’s a holiday,
Filled with funny frolics, come what may!

Luminous Nightfall Over Frozen Fields

A moose in pajamas prances proud,
Wearing a scarf, he draws a crowd.
While dancing deer join with a twirl,
They've planned a party, give it a whirl!

Snowballs fly like popcorn popped,
With giggles and snorts, they just can't stop.
They build a castle, not quite too tall,
But still, it's the funnest thing of all!

Twinkling lights from trees so bright,
Fill the fields with pure delight.
The stars above begin to wink,
As critters sit down to laugh and drink.

In this luminous nightfall, fun awaits,
With frosty friends at all the gates.
Come join the jest in this moonlit spree,
It's winter magic, wild and free!

Glistening Veils of Evening Chill

The rabbits wear shades, what a sight!
Strutting around in the pale moonlight.
Building snow forts that lean and sway,
Pretending it's summer in a wintery way!

A walrus joins, dancing on ice,
With floppy moves that are less than nice.
He slips and slides but never falls,
Making silly faces that break down walls!

The ice skates squeak with each little trip,
While laughter bursts from every lip.
Frosted flakes tickle noses so pink,
As winter friends share a warm drink!

Glistening veils bring whispers of cheer,
In this chilly world, there's nothing to fear.
So grab a sled, let’s race with delight,
Through shimmering twilight, all through the night!

Lanterns of Dusk

When dusk drops in, the cats all prance,
Trying to catch the shadows' dance.
The porch lights flicker, then they flee,
As if they're playing hide and seek with me.

The squirrels plot in the frostbit trees,
While the wind-worn leaves chuckle in the breeze.
I sip my cocoa, feeling quite keen,
As marshmallows float like a cotton candy dream.

The bikes are put away, lost to the cold,
With stories of summer now awkwardly told.
Yet here in the crunch of night’s embrace,
My laughter goes up to the moon’s round face.

So here’s to the chill that makes us all giddy,
With frost-coated jokes, so terribly witty.
As lanterns glimmer with a wink and a tease,
Let’s dance in the dark, just doing as we please.

Night's Velvet Touch

A blanket of darkness, soft as a cat,
Tucks all the world in where it’s at.
The stars are giggling behind their veil,
While owls plan pranks without fail.

The moon's cheeky shine makes shadows dance,
As mice in the bushes sneak a chance.
Wrapped in the cloak of night so neat,
Even the fireflies admit defeat.

Hot chocolate spills in this cheesy affair,
As laughter erupts in the frosty air.
So gather your friends, let stories unfold,
In the cozy embrace of the night’s bold hold.

With sleigh bells jingling in odd, funny ways,
We’ll create our own winter's silly displays.
For in the soft touch of darkness we find,
That laughter is the warmth that always shines blind.

Hues of the Dimming Horizon

The sun bows down in his favorite chair,
As blues and purples mix without a care.
The world takes a breath, and then it grins,
While the clouds play games, twirling like spins.

Even the rooftops wear colors so bright,
They'd make any rainbow squeal with delight.
Snowflakes join in with their delicate flair,
Swirling around with a foolish air.

A snowman winks with a carrot-nose glee,
While the children plot their next snowball spree.
The evening chuckles, it’s clearly a treat,
With ghosts of winter dancing on frozen street.

As the twilight dims with a laugh and a wink,
We gather our hats and grab one last drink.
Here’s to the colors that fade with a twist,
Creating a canvas that none can resist.

The Chill of Awakening Stars

Stars pop out like popcorn in skies,
Winking and giggling at startled sighs.
With constellations rehearsing their lines,
They twinkle and sparkle, oh what clever signs!

The chilly breeze sings with a playful tone,
As mittens are lost with a mischievous groan.
In this crystal night where laughter spills,
Who knew that frozen air could pay such bills?

Frosty fingers poke at the moon's soft face,
Tickling the night in this whimsical race.
The giggles of stars fill the cold air bright,
As fun takes the lead in this spirited night.

So join in the frolic, let spirits take flight,
With each frosted giggle to warm our delight.
The chill holds a charm, when laughter's the key,
Unlocking the wonders where all can be free.

Dusk's Dancing Lights

In the sky, colors clash, oh what a sight,
Snowflakes swirl in an awkward flight,
A penguin slips, with flair it lands,
While a snowman waves with carrot hands.

Cats in sweaters prance with glee,
Chasing shadows beneath the trees,
A dog in goggles laughs out loud,
As snowflakes gather, forming a crowd.

The sun takes its bow, a grand retreat,
In snowsuits, kids slip on the street,
Gentle breezes with chilly sighs,
Tickle noses and make faces rise.

Each twinkling star seems to zap,
A bear in pajamas takes a nap,
Night whispers secrets, cozy and bright,
As laughter dances in the frosty light.

Echoes of Ember and Ice

Fires crackle with a joyful cheer,
Marshmallows pop as they draw near,
Snowmen gossip on the frosty lane,
While children giggle, tossing snow again.

Socks mismatched, a fashion crime,
Frosty footprints in rhythmic rhyme,
A squirrel tries to steal a hat,
But can't quite balance and lands—kerplat!

The moon peeks in with a cheeky grin,
Reflecting laughter that bubbles within,
Ice skates twirl with goofy flair,
As graceful moves go plop, oh dear!

Warm cocoa spills with a plop and a splash,
A marshmallow dive, oh what a crash,
Echoes of laughter, a frosty delight,
Spin through the night in the soft twilight.

A Tantalizing Chill

Noses red, cheeks like apples bright,
Snowflakes tickle, what a funny sight,
Hot chocolate flows, a river wide,
With marshmallows battling on the side.

The cat in boots is on patrol,
Chasing icicles, playing the role,
While mittens fight to stay on hands,
As snowballs fly from all the lands.

A winter's breeze whispers jokes so sly,
As penguins slide on the frosty pie,
Children dash, a clumsy race,
Falling over, what a silly space!

The stars take stage, all sparkly and bright,
As giggles wrap around the night,
In the quilt of snow, watch the fun unfold,
As laughter warms against the cold.

Veiled Luminescence

Invisible giggles in the crisp night air,
With snowflakes tumbling down without a care,
A snowball fight, they throw with glee,
Watch out for snowmen, they might disagree!

Skunks in pajamas dance in the street,
While ducks in scarves try to tap their feet,
Frosty canines with goggles and flair,
Chase winter shadows that vanish in air.

Giggles echo as fireworks burst,
In chilly twilight, it feels like a thirst,
For laughter that twinkles like starlit skies,
In the whispering cold, joy never dies.

Oh, winter's charm brings a chuckle or two,
With jokes on the wind as the night bids adieu,
The world's a glow, a radiant spree,
In the blanket of twilight, filled with glee.

Reflections in a Glassy Lake

Beneath the sky, a mirror sits,
Where ducks wear hats and froggies chat.
A fish jumps high, in silly fits,
While the old otter laughs at that.

In winter's chill, the ice does squeak,
As a beaver slides all on his back.
He makes a sound, a funny squeak,
Then shows off moves that steal the knack.

The sun bows low, the light's a tease,
A squirrel juggles acorns with flair.
The icy breeze brings such a freeze,
But warmth from laughter fills the air.

As night draws close, the critters cheer,
With glowing eyes, they dance and play.
In this frozen realm, fun's sincere,
Where winter's jokes outshine the gray.

Shadows Reaching for the Stars

The shadows stretch with silly glee,
As mice attempt to climb a tree.
They slip and slide; oh what a spree!
Chasing wisps like kids set free.

A raccoon leaps, a prankster bold,
He grabs a star or so he's told.
But tumbles cause a sight to behold,
As he rolls down on paws of gold.

The owls hoot tunes that make me grin,
While rabbits hop with flopping chin.
They celebrate with cheeky spin,
In twilight's fun, the life begins.

With giggles that enchant the night,
The critters dance 'neath fading light.
Shadows stretching, quite a sight,
In this wild spree, all things are bright.

Mosaic of Twilight Colors

The sky's a canvas, splashed and bright,
With purple, pink, and shades of night.
A penguin wobbles with delight,
In colors that make him feel just right.

A fox in plaid, quite the sight,
Jumps through brush, a playful fright.
While fireflies flicker with excited light,
Chasing shadows with all their might.

The ground is set for a grand parade,
With snowmen wearing shades, unafraid.
They dance and twirl, a charade,
In hues that snap — as laughter's made.

The evening grows with antics bold,
And stories swap from young to old.
Each color sparkles, laughter told,
In this mosaic, warmth unfolds.

Silvery Guests of the Night

The silvery moon dons a funny hat,
While owls play cards with a feathered cat.
They joke and cackle, oh imagine that,
As shadows boogie in their spats.

A raccoon, dressed for a fancy gala,
Trips on a branch, 'What a great falla!'
With giggles that ripple, like a sweet salla,
Their nighttime fun's an endless ball-a.

Two hedgehogs race, each one a prince,
Through the twinkling stars, they make a spin.
With snappy moves, and no recompense,
Their laughter rings, a cheeky win.

As night birds sing their silly tune,
The silvery guests prance under moon.
In this frosty world where fun's in bloom,
They embrace the dark, it’s their big boom!

A Palette of Cold Serenity

Pine trees in sweaters, looking so proud,
Snowmen are dancing, boogieing loud.
Frosty air tickles my frozen nose,
Penguins are whispering, plotting in rows.

Icicles dangle like fancy new bling,
Squirrels wear mittens, oh what a thing!
Hot cocoa bubbles, with marshmallows too,
Winter's a party, come join the crew!

Cardigans flutter in a breezy spree,
As snowflakes twirl down, embrace the free.
Snowball fights start, but slippers are sly,
Watch your step closely, or you'll go awry!

Nature's a jester, with jokes up her sleeve,
In this cold wonderland, you'd better believe.
Laughter erupts as the first star shines,
Who knew winter's chill could come with punchlines?

Crystalline Moments at Dusk's Door

The sun bows low, dressed in colors so bright,
Snowflakes fall gently, they take off in flight.
Gingerbread houses stand proudly on display,
While penguins gossip about who will play.

Carrots and coal form smiles that gleam,
Frosted glass angels wear hats like a dream.
Hot cider bubbles, bubbling up cheer,
Churros lie waiting for folks to draw near.

Laughter erupts, as someone slips down,
Face full of snow, that’s silly but brown!
Hats fly as snowballs are launched at high speed,
Winter’s a hoot, it’s the perfect breed!

Twilight embraces with a chuckle and wink,
Chasing away shadows that start to shrink.
Giggles echo softly, the moon’s on the call,
In this silly twilight, we’re having a ball!

Ethereal Silence of the Coming Night

The evening draws closer, with tinsel in tow,
While kittens in boots dance on top of the snow.
Giggles and gasps fill the still frosty air,
As marshmallows tumble with whimsical flair.

A snowman debates with a cap in his hand,
Should he be silly or dignified, grand?
Snowflakes are whispering secrets so sweet,
As rabbits play hopscotch on icy cold feet.

The trees hold their breath, all glittery bright,
While puppies and children chase snowflakes at night.
Laughter and mischief entwined in delight,
As stars start to twinkle with great cosmic might.

So gather your friends, make the cold feel like fun,
In this peculiar twilight, the laughter's not done.
Nature's a jester, as night draws its charm,
With spirits so merry, we all sit and warm!

Gleaming Footprints in Moonlit Snow

Moonlight spills silver on the snowy lane,
As dogs in sweaters engage in a game.
Snowflakes catch giggles, a soft playful tease,
While cocoa cups bubble with warmth and with ease.

Footprints appear, but they wiggle and dance,
Little critters frolicking, taking a chance.
Frosty cheeks rosy, spirits high as a kite,
Snow angels are rolling in joyful delight.

Even the owls wink with whimsical glee,
As rabbits embark on a shiny spree.
Everyone’s laughing, both big and quite small,
In this winter wonder, there’s fun for us all!

With blankets of starlight wrapped 'round like a shawl,
Come join in the laughter, don’t hesitate, y’all!
The night holds a warmth, surprisingly bright,
In this whimsical winter, we dance with delight!

Moonlit Silences

Underneath the silvery light,
Bunnies hop and try to fight.
Snowmen wobble, losing their hats,
As penguins slide and laugh like bats.

Trees are twinkling with surprise,
Squirrels dance in oversized ties.
Laughter echoes through the chill,
While snowflakes float and dare to thrill.

Candles flicker, shadows play,
In the night, they lead astray.
A snowball sneaks, it strikes with glee,
Then laughter bursts — oh, can't you see?

So gather 'round the frosty charms,
Where every cold night reassures with arms.
The moon's a jester, bright and bold,
As tales of frost and fun unfold.

Dusk’s Ethereal Palette

Dusk creeps in with shades galore,
Orange pops and pinks explore.
The rabbits wear their finest coats,
As penguins pirouette in boats.

A cocoa spill turns into snow,
As giggles trail where children go.
The stars peek in, just to tease,
While icicles hang with frozen ease.

Chattering squirrels race the breeze,
In nutty suits, they aim to please.
Winter's charm, a circus show,
With twinkling winks in the afterglow.

The palette shifts, but laughter stays,
In this chilly dance, we play.
Snowflakes silently agree to fight,
As the dusk turns into a joyful night.

Frosted Dreams in Indigo

Indigo skies hang low and near,
A hedgehog hums, no signs of fear.
Mice skate round on tiny toes,
While giggling shadows prance and pose.

The ground is blanketed in gleam,
A world of wonder, sparks a dream.
Frosted laughter fills the air,
As dogs in sweaters dash with flair.

Snowmen sigh as flakes dissolve,
Their frosty noses can't evolve.
Candies melt in mittens tight,
While warm hot chocolate feels just right.

The twilight whispers funny tales,
Where laughter floats on snowy trails.
Behold the wonders, frosty schemes,
As we weave through our winter dreams.

A Tapestry of Winter Hues

In this tapestry where colors play,
There’s no need for winter gray.
A giggling fox in a scarf so neat,
Struts with style on frosty feet.

Sunset bows, a comic act,
The owls silently react.
Glistening snow like spilled confetti,
As friends toss snowballs, all so ready.

Ticklish frost, a chilly tease,
While scarves swirl around the trees.
Hot cider flows in a mug with cheer,
Every sip brings puns and jeers.

Laughter dances in the cold,
Wrapping us in warmth untold.
As colors blend in a winter muse,
We find the fun in all the hues.

Radiance Just Before Night

The sun waves goodbye, it's time to depart,
With a wink and a smile, it’s played its part.
Clouds gather round like a fluffy brigade,
While shadows sneak in, their patience displayed.

Squirrels in trees are now plotting their plans,
For a comedy show with acorn demands.
The world dims its lights, but the laughter stays bright,
As warm cups of cocoa embrace chilly night.

The moon starts to blush in twilight's embrace,
Wishing for company in this vast space.
Stars giggle softly, like little kids' glee,
As night creeps in, what a sight to see!

Hats off to evening, that sways like a tune,
While fireflies dance under the cheeky moon.
So let’s share a chuckle as day turns to shale,
Where humor ignites like a warm, hearty tale.

Fading Echoes of a Sun-Drenched Day

The golden rays take their last little bow,
While crickets prepare for their nightly wow.
Butterflies giggle, they flutter and play,
In the dimming light of a sun-drenched day.

There's a wind that whispers silly old jokes,
As trees shake their leaves like flamboyant folks.
The pond reflects laughter in watery hues,
As puddles get tickled by small dancing shoes.

A cat on the fence gives a curtsy and prance,
With a tail flick that sings of a daring dance.
The dusk holds its breath, but the fun doesn't fade,
As night draws near, in a jester's parade.

Worms tell tales under their earthen beds,
Of antics remembered, where all laughter spreads.
So here's to the twilight, with chuckles and cheer,
As we close the day with our favorite sneer!

The Soft Kiss of Coming Night

As the sun sips its tea, it begins to doze,
With clouds donning pajamas in gentle dose.
The world starts to yawn, its eyelids a-flutter,
While kittens conspire in the evening's utter.

A couple of frogs join the night’s little choir,
Each note a giggle, each chorus a fire.
Meanwhile, the stars put their best shoes on,
To shuffle and sway through the darkening dawn.

The moon plays peekaboo, round and so bright,
As shadows put on their funniest fight.
With each chuckle of wind, the crickets all cheer,
For the soft kiss of night is finally here!

So let’s spin in circles and dance without care,
The night's a jester with playful flair.
With laughter as warm as a cozy night’s wrap,
In the sleepy embrace of the twilight map.

Veils of Softly Falling Snow

The flakes waltz down like they're up to some glee,
Each one whispering jokes without a decree.
They pile up on noses and on little hats,
Turning folks into chuckling, snowballing cats.

A snowman is born, his eyes made of coal,
With a carrot for courage and a scarf for soul.
He stands in the yard with a grin on his face,
Spilling laughter like snowflakes, embracing the space.

The children all giggle as they tumble around,
In a flurry of fun, where joy can be found.
With sleds that go zipping and laughter that twirls,
The sound of pure happiness dances and swirls.

As night blankets softly and stars start to peep,
The world turns to canvas for dreams full of sleep.
So let's toast to the snow, with its veils of white,
As giggles blend in with the laughter of night.

Milton Keynes UK
Ingram Content Group UK Ltd.
UKHW022009131124
451149UK00013B/1074

9 789916 946176